Table of Contents

Steps for Learning Spelling Words

1. Look carefully at the spelling word.

2. Say the spelling word out loud.
   - How many syllables do you hear?
   - What consonant sounds do you hear?
   - What vowel sounds do you hear?

3. Check the spelling word for spelling patterns.

4. Spell the spelling word out loud.

5. Cover the spelling word.

6. Write the spelling word from memory.

7. Check the spelling word.

8. Repeat as needed.

Say each word out loud. Listen for the short *a* sound.
Copy and spell each word three times using colours of your choice.

1. cap _____ _____ _____

2. had _____ _____ _____

3. and _____ _____ _____

4. sat _____ _____ _____

5. pan _____ _____ _____

6. lap _____ _____ _____

7. jam _____ _____ _____

8. hat _____ _____ _____

9. yam _____ _____ _____

10. can _____ _____ _____

Brain Stretch

- Create a word search puzzle based on the spelling words.
- On a piece of paper, write a sentence using each spelling word.

and	can	cap	had	hat
jam	lap	pan	sat	yam

1. Fill in the blank using the best spelling word from the list.

a)   Jim _____ Tammy shared an apple for a snack..

b)   A red _____ was rolling down the road.

c)   My father makes eggs in a frying _____.

d)   We _____ on the floor and listened to the story.

e)   Grandma's _____ is growing roots on the counter.

f)   Fluffy is curled up in my _____ sleeping.

g)   John wears a striped baseball _____.

h)   My _____ blew off my head in the strong wind.

i)   Ann's favourite lunch is peanut butter and _____ .

j)   I _____ two marbles this morning, but I lost one.

Brain Stretch

How many spelling words can you fit into one sentence and still make sense? Give it a try!

1. Unscramble the spelling words.

   a) tah _____   b) tsa _____

   c) hda _____   d) maj _____

   e) pca _____   f) adn _____

   g) apn _____   h) amy _____

   i) pla _____   j) cna _____

2. Write the spelling words that rhyme with the words in each group.

   a) ham   ram   tam   _____

   b) man   fan   tan   _____

   c) cat   rat   bat   _____

   d) zap   tap   map   _____

Spelling Week 2 – Words with a Short *i* Sound

Say each word out loud. Listen for the short *i* sound.
Copy and spell each word three times using colours of your choice.

1. his   _____   _____   _____

2. him   _____   _____   _____

3. if   _____   _____   _____

4. big   _____   _____   _____

5. pin   _____   _____   _____

6. fix   _____   _____   _____

7. will   _____   _____   _____

8. win   _____   _____   _____

9. dig   _____   _____   _____

10. pit   _____   _____   _____

Brain Stretch

- Create a word search puzzle based on the spelling words.
- On a piece of paper, write a sentence using each spelling word.

Spelling Week 2 – Words with a Short *i* Sound

big	dig	fix	him	his
if	pin	pit	will	win

1. Fill in the blank using the best spelling word from the list.

a) My older sister's shoes are way too _____ for me.

b) Dad has to _____ the squeaky door.

c) I hope I _____ the draw at school today!

d) Cindy wonders _____ it will be sunny tomorrow.

e) The squirrel ran away with my peach _____.

f) Bob's brother oiled the chain on _____ bike.

g) Our dog will _____ a hole to bury her bone.

h) We played _____ the tail on the donkey.

i) When _____ summer vacation start?

j) Grandpa hugged me and I hugged _____ back.

Brain Stretch

How many spelling words can you fit into one sentence and still make sense? Give it a try!

1. Read all the words in each row. Circle all the words that rhyme.

    a)   big   fig   split   tip   rig

    b)   sip   will   pit   spill   bill

    c)   pin   sad   skin   if   win

    d)   him   pit   get   mitt   same

    e)   fix   pitch   mitt   mix   imp

    f)   fizz   man   his   whiz   lamb

2. A **synonym** is a word that means the same as another word.
    Circle the synonym for the bolded word.

    a)   **big**   fast   large   b)   **fix**   scare   mend

    c)   **pit**   hole   sit   d)   **pin**   paint   tack

3. An **antonym** is a word that has the opposite meaning of another
    word. Circle the antonym for the bolded word.

    a)   **big**   tiny   huge   b)   **win**   lose   dislike

    c)   **fix**   air   break   d)   **pit**   sail   hill

Say each word out loud. Listen for the short **o** sound.
Copy and spell each word three times using colours of your choice.

1. onto _____ _____ _____

2. hot _____ _____ _____

3. dog _____ _____ _____

4. cob _____ _____ _____

5. box _____ _____ _____

6. off _____ _____ _____

7. stop _____ _____ _____

8. lost _____ _____ _____

9. fog _____ _____ _____

10. job _____ _____ _____

Brain Stretch

- Create a word search puzzle based on the spelling words.
- On a piece of paper, write a sentence using each spelling word.

box	cob	dog	fog	hot
job	lost	off	onto	stop

1. Fill in the blank using the best spelling word from the list.

a)   We are taking care of my uncle's _____ Max this week.

b)   A thick, white _____ rolled in off the ocean.

c)   Cam _____ his favourite pencil!

d)   The sun is very _____ in summer.

e)   What kind of _____ do you want to do when you grow up?

f)   Always turn the lights _____ when you leave a room.

g)   Our cat always jumps _____ the kitchen chairs.

h)   I drank water, but could not _____ my hiccups.

i)   Mom loves to make corn on the _____ in the fall.

j)   Grandma brought us a big _____ of crayons.

Brain Stretch

How many spelling words can you fit into one sentence and still make sense? Give it a try!

1. Write in the missing letter or letters from these spelling words.

   a)   c____   b)   o____f   c)   s_____p   d) l____s____

   e)   ____n____o   f) ____ox   g)   j____b   h) f____

2. These words have a short **o** sound. Draw a line from the first part of
   the word to the second part. Print the words on the lines below.

   a)   p   op

   b)   s   ox

   c)   t   oll

   d)   st   ot

   e)   f   ock

   f)   d   oss

   a) _____   b) _____   c) _____

   d) _____   e) _____   f) _____

Spelling Week 4 – Words with a Short *u* Sound

Say each word out loud. Listen for the short *u* sound.

Copy and spell each word three times using colours of your choice.

1. up _____ _____ _____

2. bus _____ _____ _____

3. hug _____ _____ _____

4. run _____ _____ _____

5. us _____ _____ _____

6. but _____ _____ _____

7. cut _____ _____ _____

8. fun _____ _____ _____

9. must _____ _____ _____

10. jug _____ _____ _____

Brain Stretch

- Create a word search puzzle based on the spelling words.
- On a piece of paper, write a sentence using each spelling word.

Spelling Week 4 – Words with a Short *u* Sound

bus	but	cut	fun	hug
jug	must	up	us	run

1. Fill in the blank using the best spelling word from the list.

   a)   My neighbour had to _____ for the bus this morning.

   b)   My sister wants to get her hair _____ short.

   c)   This toy bunny has arms that _____ me.

   d)   Sam _____ remember to take his project to school.

   e)   Carla gets _____ at 7:30 every morning.

   f)   I hope we have a lot of _____ on our camping trip.

   g)   My uncle brought a _____ of lemonade to the picnic.

   h)   This _____ will take us right to the mall.

   i)   I like my red runners, _____ I like the blue ones better.

   j)   Grandpa brought _____ some colouring books.

Brain Stretch

How many spelling words can you fit into one sentence and still make sense? Give it a try!

1. Circle the words that do <u>not</u> have a short **u** sound.

a) bunch   cough   tune   lung   putter

b) round   fluffy   bounce   tumble   rust

c) sun   pounce   beauty   butter   swung

d) grouch   pump   rumble   rough   guess

e) luck   fuss   comb   fudge   about

2. Make a word with the short **u** sound. Try the letters given.
   Choose the right letter or letters. Write them on the line beside the
   rest of the word.

Example: bl   st   fr   <u>st</u>umble

c   b   gl   j   l   fl   cl   st   r

a) **f   l   st** ____umber   b) **f   c   s** ____over

c) **r   c   b** ____ough   d) **h   j   r** ____udge

e) **gl   fl   cl** ____uff   f) **g   b   t** ____ump

g) **t   c   gr** ____ouch   h) **d   m   b** ____ubble

Spelling Week 5 – Words with a Short *e* Sound

Say each word out loud. Listen for the short *e* sound.
Copy and spell each word three times using colours of your choice.

1. red _____ _____ _____

2. leg _____ _____ _____

3. tell _____ _____ _____

4. yes _____ _____ _____

5. went _____ _____ _____

6. bed _____ _____ _____

7. let _____ _____ _____

8. wet _____ _____ _____

9. end _____ _____ _____

10. best _____ _____ _____

Brain Stretch

- Create a word search puzzle based on the spelling words.
- On a piece of paper, write a sentence using each spelling word.

bed	best	end	leg	let
red	tell	went	wet	yes

1. Fill in the blank using the best spelling word from the list.

a) My cousins and my family all _____ to the zoo Saturday.

b) I get an allowance if I make my _____ every day.

c) Patty was so sad when she got to the _____ of her book.

d) Jack wants to _____ us a funny joke he heard.

e) Dogs and cats can often be _____ friends.

f) Kathy stepped in a puddle and her foot got all _____ .

g) Grandma said _____ to a trip to the ice cream store.

h) I bumped my knee and it turned really _____ .

i) My aunt _____ me help her make salad for dinner..

j) A mosquito bit me on the _____, right by my knee.

Brain Stretch

How many spelling words can you fit into one sentence and still make sense? Give it a try!

1. Underline the word with the short **e** sound.
   Write the word on the line.

   a) chick   better   sill   rose   life   _____

   b) skill   click   bread   clover   mass   _____

   c) man   wrote   fuzz   fit   shed   _____

   d) crash   mend   marry   fist   calf   _____

   e) mean   fear   spine   said   scarf   _____

2. Circle the word with the short **e** sound that makes the most sense.
   Write the word in the sentence.

   a) Terry _____ to the store to buy milk. (meant   went)

   b) Yu took her _____ painting to the art contest. (pet's   best)

   c) My brother _____ a book about bears. (read   red)

   d) Carrie has a fly bite on her _____. (neck   vest)

   e) Sal bought a _____ of colour pencils for school. (net   set)

   f) We built a _____ to keep our dog in the backyard. (net   fence)

Say each word out loud. Listen for the long *a* sound.
Copy and spell each word three times using colours of your choice.

1. save _____ _____ _____

2. page _____ _____ _____

3. today _____ _____ _____

4. wait _____ _____ _____

5. stay _____ _____ _____

6. sale _____ _____ _____

7. play _____ _____ _____

8. rain _____ _____ _____

9. game _____ _____ _____

10. take _____ _____ _____

Spelling Tips: The long *a* sound can be spelled with
- letters *ai* (*pail*)
- letter *a* with a **consonant** + *e* (*cake*)
- letters *ay* (*bay*)

game	page	play	rain	sale
save	stay	take	today	wait

1. Fill in the blank using the best spelling word from the list.

   a) Patty and I are going to _____ over at Sue's house tonight.

   b) I can't _____ for Sam's birthday!

   c) Cami's baby sister drew all over the book _____!

   d) I want to play the new board _____ we got.

   e) If _____ my money, I can buy a new bike someday.

   f) Mom likes to buy things cheap when they go on _____.

   g) _____, we are going to the dentist for a checkup.

   h) To _____ this game, you have to guess what I'm drawing.

   i) My neighbour asked if we could _____ his dog for a walk.

   j) The sky is very grey. It looks like it will _____ soon.

Brain Stretch

How many spelling words can you fit into one sentence and still make sense? Give it a try!

1. Say the word out loud. Underline the words with the long **a** sound.

   a) break   late   seat   wait   reach

   b) lace   watch   hazy   peace   crate

   c) waste   beat   grape   face   boat

   d) real   sway   make   cap   grey

   e) green   may   star   gate   eight

2. Write the letters of the alphabet that have a long **a** sound in their name.

_____

3. Write the numbers between 1 and 100 that have a long **a** sound in their name.

_____

_____

4. Write as many words as you can that rhyme with **play**.

_____

_____

Say each word out loud. Look at the different letters that make the long *e* sound. Copy and spell each word three times using colours of your choice.

1. keep   _____ _____ _____

2. dream _____ _____ _____

3. eat   _____ _____ _____

4. three   _____ _____ _____

5. easy   _____ _____ _____

6. need   _____ _____ _____

7. meet   _____ _____ _____

8. read   _____ _____ _____

9. each   _____ _____ _____

10. mean _____ _____ _____

Spelling Tips: The long *e* sound can be spelled with

- letter *e* by itself, and *e* followed by a **consonant + e** (*evil, even*)
- letters *ee, ea,* and *ie* (*feel, spear, field*)
- letter *y* (*kitty*)

dream	each	easy	eat	keep
mean	meet	need	read	three

1. Fill in the blank using the best spelling word from the list.

a) Someday, I want to _____ a real-life astronaut.

b) It is cold outside, so I _____ to wear my mittens today.

c) Our dog gave birth to _____ puppies yesterday.

d) Tom wants to _____ all the Harry Potter books.

e) The _____ witch turned the prince into a frog.

f) I _____ my favourite things in a special box in my room.

g) Chris shared his marbles, and we got 6 marbles _____.

h) Mary said her spelling test was _____ this week.

i) I had a _____ that I rode on a rainbow unicorn.

j) Every day after school, I _____ a snack when I get home.

Brain Stretch

How many spelling words can you fit into one sentence and still make sense? Give it a try!

1. Read all the words in each row. Circle all the words that rhyme.

   a)   bee   flea   sap   tea   ask

   b)   had   meat   cat   wheat   fleet

   c)   team   game   seem   mean   beam

   d)   heat   pat   street   sheet   seat

   e)   feel   pale   leap   meal   seal

   f)   life   reef   leaf   whiff   thief

2. A **synonym** is a word that means the same as another word.
   Circle the synonym for the bolded word.

   a)   **mean**   fair   unkind   b)   **eat**   lunch   munch

   c)   **tiny**   huge   small   d)   **leave** visit   go

3. An **antonym** is a word that has the opposite meaning of another
   word. Circle the antonym for the bolded word.

   a)   **sweet** chewy   sour   b)   **weak**   strong   slim

   c)   **tody**   messy   nest   d)   **below** under   above

4. How many syllables does the word have? Write the number on the line.

   a)   extreme _____   b)   sleep _____   c)   jellybean _____

Say each word out loud. Listen for the long *i* sound.
Copy and spell each word three times using colours of your choice.

1. pie   _____   _____   _____

2. tight   _____   _____   _____

3. kind   _____   _____   _____

4. time   _____   _____   _____

5. night   _____   _____   _____

6. bite   _____   _____   _____

7. write   _____   _____   _____

8. high   _____   _____   _____

9. right   _____   _____   _____

10. pine   _____   _____   _____

Spelling Tips: The long *i* sound can be spelled with
- letters *igh* and *ign* (*bright, design*)
- letter *i* followed by **consonant + e** (*dive*)
- letters *ie* and *y* (*pie, buy*)

bite	high	kind	night	pie
pine	right	tight	time	write

1. Fill in the blank using the best spelling word from the list.

   a)   I study for my tests so I can get the answers _____ .

   b)   My pet rabbit Henry wants a _____ of my carrot.

   c)   Mom said it is _____ to leave for school.

   d)   Dad made his first apple _____ on the weekend.

   e)   I am growing and now my shoes are too _____.

   f)   Miss Smith asked the class to _____ a funny story.

   g)   The evergreen tree in our yard is a white _____.

   h)   You should always be _____ to animals.

   i)   My kite is stuck way up _____ in that tree.

   j)   The world becomes very quiet at _____.

Brain Stretch

How many spelling words can you fit into one sentence and still make sense? Give it a try!

1. Say the word out loud. Underline the words with the long *i* sound.

a)	spine	pink	skit	guy	fly
b)	time	kind	iron	skin	thin
c)	skill	slip	ripe	eye	twist
d)	mine	grime	twice	lip	while
e)	rind	grit	sink	pail	wipe
f)	lime	sting	rhyme	bit	lie

2. Circle the word with the short *e* sound that makes the most sense.
   Write the word in the sentence.

   a)   I had a bad cold last week, but now I'm _____. (crying   fine)

   b)   We can play one more game if we have _____. (time   limes)

   c)   Mom was in the garden and got dirt in her _____. (spine   eye)

   d)   A ruler helps me to draw a straight _____. (line   slide)

   e)   Our cat likes to sleep in the _____. (sunshine   slime)

   f)   My pet hamster likes to _____ inside my sleeve. (climb   rhyme)

3. Write the number words from one to ten that have a long *i* sound.

_____

Say each word out loud. Listen for the long *i* and long *e* sounds.
Copy and spell each word three times using colours of your choice.

1. cry _____ _____ _____

2. baby _____ _____ _____

3. try _____ _____ _____

4. any _____ _____ _____

5. only _____ _____ _____

6. why _____ _____ _____

7. many _____ _____ _____

8. story _____ _____ _____

9. very _____ _____ _____

10. fly _____ _____ _____

Brain Stretch

- Create a word search puzzle based on the spelling words.
- On a piece of paper, write a sentence using each spelling word.

any	baby	cry	fly	many
only	story	try	very	why

1. Fill in the blank using the best spelling word from the list.

   a)   Whenever I do something new, I always _____ my very best.

   b)   The Elder told us the _____ of Turtle Island.

   c)   Most of the time, I am a _____ active person.

   d)   Ellen does not know _____ she sneezes so often.

   e)   Jim ate four cookies, but I _____ ate one.

   f)   A _____ is buzzing around and bugging the cat.

   g)   We have gone to the lake _____ times since I was little.

   h)   Do you have _____ spare paper you can give me?

   i)   My aunt just brought over her new _____ for us to meet.

   j)   Some people _____ when they are sad and when they are happy.

Brain Stretch

How many spelling words can you fit into one sentence and still make sense? Give it a try!

1. Read the sentence clue. Unscramble the word and write it in the space.

   a) Our dog has lots of toys, but he _____ plays with one. (yoln)

   b) Grandpa told us a _____ about his life on the farm. (tysor)

   c) Kim's baby did not _____ when he was born. (rcy)

   d) Birds _____ away very fast when a hawk comes around. (fyl)

   e) The dog chased the hen, and now she is _____ angry. (revy)

   f) My little brother wants to _____ ice skating. (ryt)

2. A compound word is a big word that is made up of two smaller words put together. Write the two words that make the bigger word.

   Example: evergreen = ever + green

   a) frypan = _____   b) daytime = _____

   c) horsefly = _____   d) jellybean = _____

   e) eyeball = _____   f) sunset = _____

Spelling Week 10 – Words with a Long *o* Sound

Say each word out loud. Look at the different letters that make the long **o** sound. Copy and spell each word three times using colours of your choice.

1. road _____ _____ _____

2. snow _____ _____ _____

3. hope _____ _____ _____

4. also _____ _____ _____

5. glow _____ _____ _____

6. goal _____ _____ _____

7. throw _____ _____ _____

8. soap _____ _____ _____

9. nose _____ _____ _____

10. follow _____ _____ _____

Spelling Tips: A long **o** sound can be made with

- letter **o** (*troll, comb, go*)
- letters **oe** (*toe*)
- letters **oa** and **ow** (*boat, glow*)
- letter **o** followed by a **consonant + e** (*mole*)

also	follow	glow	goal	hope
nose	road	snow	soap	throw

1. Fill in the blank using the best spelling word from the list.

a) I love to play in the _____ in winter time.

b) My baby sister's favourite game is _____ the leader.

c) We have a cat, but we _____ have a bird and a dog.

d) My new shoelaces _____ in the dark!

e) I wash my hands with _____ and water before I eat.

f) Dad is teaching my sister how to _____ a baseball.

g) My grandparents live just down the _____ from us.

h) A healthy dog's _____ is always cold and wet.

i) My sister scored the winning _____ in soccer today!

j) I _____ it will be sunny for our picnic tomorrow.

Brain Stretch

How many spelling words can you fit into one sentence and still make sense? Give it a try!

1. Circle the words that do **not** have the long **o** sound.

a)   tower   goat   robe   lower   clock

b)   port   robot   sock   post   work

c)   soak   torn   book   toss   toast

d)   form   pool   more   slop   wrote

2. Write a word that uses the same letters to make the long **o** sound. Say the word out. Do **not** use spelling words.

a) **ore** _____   b) **oa** _____

c) **ow** _____   d) **ort** _____

3. How many syllables does the word have? Write the number on the line.

a)   swallow _____   b)   tomorrow _____   c)   float _____

4. Use the list below to make three compound words. Say two words together to see if they make sense. Write the compound word on the line.

no   snow   corn   where   flake   pop

a)   _____   b)   _____   c)   _____

Say each word out loud. Listen for the long and short *oo* sounds.
Copy and spell each word three times using colours of your choice.

1. book _____ _____ _____

2. took _____ _____ _____

3. food _____ _____ _____

4. cook _____ _____ _____

5. clue _____ _____ _____

6. school _____ _____ _____

7. threw _____ _____ _____

8. crew _____ _____ _____

9. soon _____ _____ _____

10. should _____ _____ _____

Spelling Tips

The long *oo* sound can be spelled with
- letters *ew* (*grew*) and *ue* (*blue*)
- letters *oo* (*pool*) and *ough* (*through*)
- letter *u* with **consonant + e** (*tune*)

The short *oo* sound can be spelled with
- letters *oo* (*look*)
- letters *ou* (*would*)

book	clue	cook	crew	food
school	should	soon	threw	took

1. Fill in the blank using the best spelling word from the list.

   a) A big _____ of workers came to put shingles on our roof.

   b) I walk to _____ with my big brother and my friends.

   c) You _____ always say please and thank you.

   d) My mother _____ the ball for our dog Max to fetch.

   e) Grandma _____ photos of me and my family.

   f) My cousin will _____ be 10 years old.

   g) Hanna's favourite _____ is *Green Eggs and Ham.*

   h) I want to learn to _____ grilled cheese sandwiches.

   i) Our dog Max always knows when someone is eating _____.

   j) The detective solved the mystery when he saw the _____.

Brain Stretch

How many spelling words can you fit into one sentence and still make sense? Give it a try!

1. Circle the words that have a long **oo** sound.

   a)   flew   shook   boom   due   toe

   b)   room   cow   fruit   wool   boot

   c)   tool   flute   sport   took   mood

   d)   bloom   from   good   rule   soup

2. Underline the words that have a short **oo** sound.

   a)   spool   look   tool   soot   wool

   b)   tuna   stood   foot   tooth   shook

   c)   loop   brook   moon   book   loop

   d)   zoom   wood   fool   crook   could

3. Write the correct letter beside the word.
   Write **S** for a short **oo** sound. Write **L** for a long **oo** sound.

   a)   book ____   b)   grew ____   c)   cruel ____   d)   woof ____

   e)   hoof ____   f)   fool ____   g)   spoon ____   h)   crook ____

   i)   glue ____   j)   should ____   k)   June ____   l)   wool ____

Say each word out loud. Think about what letter or letters are missing. Copy and spell each word three times using colours of your choice.

1. bark _____ _____ _____

2. party _____ _____ _____

3. yard _____ _____ _____

4. barn _____ _____ _____

5. farm _____ _____ _____

6. hard _____ _____ _____

7. star _____ _____ _____

8. dark _____ _____ _____

9. card _____ _____ _____

10. mark _____ _____ _____

Brain Stretch

- Create a word search puzzle based on the spelling words.
- On a piece of paper, write a sentence using each spelling word.

bark	barn	card	dark	farm
hard	mark	party	star	yard

1. Fill in the blank using the best spelling word from the list.

   a) My uncle keeps horses and a donkey in his new _____ .

   b) I got a funny Valentine _____ from my friend.

   c) Donna got a high _____ on her math test.

   d) In winter, it gets _____ a lot earlier in the evenings.

   e) A hungry skunk dug holes all over our _____ .

   f) Our teacher gives us a _____ for passing our spelling test.

   g) The back gate is rusty and it is _____ to open.

   h) Open the door quietly or the dog will _____ .

   i) This weekend, I'm going to Jenny's birthday _____ .

   j) I love to visit my uncle's _____ to see all the animals.

Brain Stretch

How many spelling words can you fit into one sentence and still make sense? Give it a try!

1. Write the words below in alphabetical order on the lines.

park   sharp   card   far   apart   hare

a) _____   b) _____   c) _____

d) _____   e) _____   f) _____

2. Write a short sentence using the word below.

a) care _____

b) share _____

c) shark _____

d) part _____

e) large _____

f) stare _____

g) guard _____

Say each word out loud. Listen to how the letters blend smoothly with **s**.
Copy and spell each word three times using colours of your choice.

1. skip _____ _____ _____

2. smart _____ _____ _____

3. just _____ _____ _____

4. still _____ _____ _____

5. snack _____ _____ _____

6. smell _____ _____ _____

7. spill _____ _____ _____

8. swim _____ _____ _____

9. scarf _____ _____ _____

10. slip _____ _____ _____

Brain Stretch

- Create a word search puzzle based on the spelling words.
- On a piece of paper, write a sentence using each spelling word.

just	scarf	skip	slip	smart
smell	snack	spill	still	swim

1. Fill in the blank using the best spelling word from the list.

a)   The rabbit sits very _____ so you won't see him.

b)   My friend and I were hungry so we got a _____.

c)   Frank is very _____ and good at math.

d)   When I'm happy, I like to _____ everywhere.

e)   I love the _____ of flowers.

f)   Mom _____ sat down to eat lunch when the phone rang.

g)   Sami is pouring the milk carefully so he does not _____ it.

h)   Be careful you don't _____ on the ice!

i)   Our fish like to _____ through the gaps in the rocks.

j)   It is windy and cold out today so I will wear my warm _____.

Brain Stretch

How many spelling words can you fit into one sentence and still make sense? Give it a try!

1. Write a word that has the **s** blend below. The **s** blend can start the word, end the word, or be inside the word. Do **not** use any words we have spelled this week.

   a) sk _____

   b) sl _____

   c) sm _____

   d) sp _____

   e) sc _____

   f) sw _____

   g) st _____

   h) sn _____

2. Find the **s** blend in the word. Write the **s** blend on the line.

   a) first _____   b) snip _____   c) risk _____   d) hassle _____

   e) sweat _____   f) splat _____   g) snail _____   h) castle _____

3. A **synonym** is a word that means the same as another word. Circle the synonym for the bolded word.

   a) **spare**   extra   loose   b) **start**   stop   begin

4. An **antonym** is a word that has the opposite meaning of another word. Circle the antonym for the bolded word.

   a) **slip**   smooth   stick   b) **scared**   brave   lost

Spelling Week 14 – Words with *r* Blends

Say each word out loud. Listen to how the letters blend smoothly with the **r**. Copy and spell each word three times using colours of your choice.

1. from _____ _____ _____

2. crab _____ _____ _____

3. drip _____ _____ _____

4. brush _____ _____ _____

5. bring _____ _____ _____

6. grab _____ _____ _____

7. trip _____ _____ _____

8. pretty _____ _____ _____

9. tree _____ _____ _____

10. frog _____ _____ _____

Brain Stretch

- Create a word search puzzle based on the spelling words.
- On a piece of paper, write a sentence using each spelling word.

bring	brush	crab	drip	frog
from	grab	pretty	tree	trip

1. Fill in the blank using the best spelling word from the list.

a) We planted a red maple _____ in our backyard.

b) My baby sister tries to _____ everyone's hair.

c) The flowers in our garden are very _____.

d) Be careful that you don't _____ over the hose!

e) This package is _____ my grandparents.

f) We're going to _____ watermelon to the barbecue.

g) We saw a blue _____ on the shore by the ocean.

h) I _____ my dog's hair every week to keep it neat.

i) The kitchen tap needs to be fixed. It's starting to _____.

j) Can you see the green _____ peeking out of the pond?

Brain Stretch

How many spelling words can you fit into one sentence and still make sense? Give it a try!

1. Draw or cut out and paste a picture to show the meaning of the word.

crack	brush
tree	crab
drip	grab

Say each word out loud. Look at where **sh** sound can be in a word. Copy and spell each word three times using colours of your choice.

1. push _____ _____ _____

2. trash _____ _____ _____

3. dish _____ _____ _____

4. shake _____ _____ _____

5. wish _____ _____ _____

6. share _____ _____ _____

7. fresh _____ _____ _____

8. shell _____ _____ _____

9. washer _____ _____ _____

10. brush _____ _____ _____

Brain Stretch

- Create a word search puzzle based on the spelling words.
- On a piece of paper, write a sentence using each spelling word.

Spelling Week 15 – Words in the *sh* Family

brush	dish	fresh	rush	shake
share	shell	trash	washer	wish

1. Fill in the blank using the best spelling word from the list.

    a)   I found a pretty clam _____ on the beach.

    b)   We always pick up any _____ we find at the park.

    c)   Mom said she would _____ her sandwich with me.

    d)   Marty washed that _____ but it is still dirty.

    e)   I _____ I could have a unicorn for a pet.

    f)   The cat purrs loudly when I _____ her fur.

    g)   My uncle Ted is a window _____.

    h)   If a door won't open when you _____ it, try pulling it.

    i)   The train going by caused everything to rattle and _____.

    j)   Dad made a salad with _____ lettuce and tomato.

Brain Stretch

How many spelling words can you fit into one sentence and still make sense? Give it a try!

Spelling Week 15 – Word Study

1. Ask permission to use a magazine or newspaper for this activity.
   Cut out letters to spell the word below.
   Glue or tape the letters in the correct order in the box.

shirt	push
shine	brush
slush	shift
wish	hush

Spelling Week 16 – Words in the *ck* Family

Say each word out loud. Listen for the sound **ck** makes.

Copy and spell each word three times using colours of your choice.

1. sock   _____   _____   _____

2. quack   _____   _____   _____

3. luck   _____   _____   _____

4. pick   _____   _____   _____

5. clock   _____   _____   _____

6. neck   _____   _____   _____

7. pack   _____   _____   _____

8. deck   _____   _____   _____

9. rock   _____   _____   _____

10. flick   _____   _____   _____

Brain Stretch

- Create a word search puzzle based on the spelling words.
- On a piece of paper, write a sentence using each spelling word.

clock	deck	flick	luck	neck
pack	pick	quack	rock	sock

1. Fill in the blank using the best spelling word from the list.

a) My family is going to _____ strawberries this weekend.

b) I have a really nice _____ collection.

c) The ducks on the pond _____ loudly when we have food.

d) We're eating dinner out on the _____ today.

e) Mom is going to _____ my lunch for school tomorrow.

f) The _____ has stopped. It needs a new battery.

g) I has lost my favourite striped _____.

h) Horses _____ their tails to swat away pesky flies.

i) I found a four-leaf clover! Now I will have good _____!

j) A giraffe has a very long _____ so it can reach leaves.

Brain Stretch

How many spelling words can you fit into one sentence and still make sense? Give it a try!

Spelling Week 16 – Word Study

1. Draw and colour a picture of the object or thing.

clock	sock
duck	backpack
stick	rock

Say each word out loud. Think about what these words have in common. Copy and spell each word three times using colours of your choice.

1. which _____ _____ _____

2. what _____ _____ _____

3. there _____ _____ _____

4. where _____ _____ _____

5. both _____ _____ _____

6. who _____ _____ _____

7. that _____ _____ _____

8. when _____ _____ _____

9. this _____ _____ _____

10. those _____ _____ _____

Did you notice anything about the spelling words? Some of the words are question words.
Examples: Who is...?   What is...?   When are...?   Where did...?

Some of the words help to give answers.
Examples: This book...   That drawing...   Those toys...

both	that	there	this	those
what	when	which	who	where

1. Fill in the blank using the best spelling word from the list.

a) _____ is my sweater over there on the couch.

b) _____ is your favourite food?

c) My brothers _____ like to play hockey.

d) I know that place. I went _____ for ballet lessons.

e) Our neighbours gave us _____ pretty plants over there.

f) _____ wants to watch a movie after dinner?

g) _____ are we going to the library?

h) _____ of these books do you want to read next?

i) _____ did you put that empty box?

j) _____ is what I want to plant in the vegetable garden.

Brain Stretch

How many spelling words can you fit into one sentence and still make sense? Give it a try!

Some of the spelling words are question words. Other words help to give answers.

1. Read the question. Write the correct question word from the list.

what   when   where   who   why   which   how

a) _____ left the door open?

b) _____ is the kitchen floor so slippery?

c) _____ is Grandma coming over?

d) _____ did you do on your spelling test?

e) _____ of these cups belongs to you?

f) _____ is the name of this song?

g) _____ did I leave my glasses?

2. Read the question. Write the correct answer word from the list.

then   there   this   that   those   these

a) Where did Jack sit? He sat _____.

b) What happened next? _____ she left the house.

c) What is in your hand? _____ are marbles.

d) What was that noise? _____ was my stomach.

e) Which ball do you want? I want _____ orange ball.

f) Which are you buying? I'm buying _____ blue flowers.

Spelling Week 18 – Words in the *ch* and *tch* Families

Say each word out loud. The letters **ch** and **tch** can make the same sound. Copy and spell each word three times using colours of your choice.

1. chin   _____ _____ _____

2. witch   _____ _____ _____

3. much   _____ _____ _____

4. catch   _____ _____ _____

5. chat   _____ _____ _____

6. lunch   _____ _____ _____

7. chick   _____ _____ _____

8. itch   _____ _____ _____

9. watch   _____ _____ _____

10. match   _____ _____ _____

Brain Stretch

- Create a word search puzzle based on the spelling words.
- On a piece of paper, write a sentence using each spelling word.

catch	chat	chick	chin	itch
lunch	match	much	watch	witch

1. Fill in the blank using the best spelling word from the list.

a)   My sister likes to wear socks that don't _____ .

b)   The hen made soft clucking sounds at her baby _____.

c)   _____ me! I can do a cartwheel!

d)   The _____ in the story locked the boy in a cage.

e)   Our old dog does not play with his toys as _____ now.

f)   Santa Claus has a white beard on his _____.

g)   My mother likes to _____ with our neighbour Pat.

h)   I wonder what we are having for _____ today.

i)   The man uses a net to _____ butterflies to study.

j)   She likes to _____ ants take bits of food she gives them.

Brain Stretch

How many spelling words can you fit into one sentence and still make sense? Give it a try!

Spelling Week 18 – Word Study

1. Sort these words into the correct column. Write them in the table below.

chance	chill	crunch	finch
hatch	latch	march	match
munch	patch	pinch	pitch
ranch	sketch	stitch	watch

Words with *ch*	Words with *tch*

2. Read all the words. Circle the words that do **not** belong.

chest   patch   shout   school   month   match   where

Say each word out loud.

Copy and spell each word three times using colours of your choice.

1. one   _____   _____   _____

2. two   _____   _____   _____

3. three   _____   _____   _____

4. four   _____   _____   _____

5. five   _____   _____   _____

6. six   _____   _____   _____

7. seven   _____   _____   _____

8. eight   _____   _____   _____

9. nine   _____   _____   _____

10. ten   _____   _____   _____

Brain Stretch

- Create a word search puzzle based on the spelling words.
- On a piece of paper, write a sentence using each spelling word.

eight	five	four	nine	one
seven	six	ten	three	two

1. Fill in the blank using the best spelling word from the list. Read the questions carefully.

    a)   The word **unique** means that something is _____ of a kind.

    b)   My brother is twelve. He is twice my age. How old am I? _____

    c)   We have _____ fingers and _____ toes.

    d)   There are _____ days in a week.

    e)   We made twelve muffins. We ate two. How many are left? _____

    f)   We sang the song about _____ blind mice.

    g)   Identical twins are _____ people who look exactly alike.

    h)   We had twelve eggs. Mom cooked four. How many are left? _____

    i)   I am less than six but more than four. How old am I? _____

    j)   My finger has a cut on it. How many fingers do not have a cut? _____

Brain Stretch

How many spelling words can you fit into one sentence and still make sense? Give it a try!

Spelling Week 19 – Word Study

1. Sort the number words into numerical order. Write the number words in the table in the correct order.

Example:	fifteen	nineteen	eight	twelve
	eight	twelve	fifteen	nineteen

a) thirteen	seven	eleven	twenty	four

b) twelve	nine	five	seventeen	one

2. Put the number words in alphabetical order. Write the number words in the table in the correct order.

a) fourteen	nine	six	twenty	eight

b) sixteen	two	five	nineteen	eighteen

Say each word out loud. Some of the words are times of the day. Copy and spell each word three times using colours of your choice.

1. Monday _____ _____ _____

2. Tuesday _____ _____ _____

3. Wednesday _____ _____ _____

4. Thursday _____ _____ _____

5. Friday _____ _____ _____

6. Saturday _____ _____ _____

7. Sunday _____ _____ _____

8. morning _____ _____ _____

9. afternoon _____ _____ _____

10. night _____ _____ _____

Brain Stretch

- Create a word search puzzle based on the spelling words.
- On a piece of paper, write a sentence using each spelling word.

afternoon   Friday   Monday   morning   night

Saturday   Sunday   Thursday   Tuesday   Wednesday

1. Fill in the blank using the best spelling word from the list.

a) _____ is the last day of the school week.

b) The middle day of the week is _____.

c) People get ready for school and work in the _____.

d) _____ is usually a fun day for most people.

e) Which day name starts with the sound of "two"? _____

f) Children get home from school each day in the _____.

g) _____ is the day many people go to church.

h) _____ is the time for homework, dinner, and sleep.

i) Which day of the week comes before Friday? _____

j) _____ is the first day of the school and work week.

Brain Stretch

How many spelling words can you fit into one sentence and still make sense? Give it a try!

1. This is a very old poem. A long time ago, people thought a child's personality was decided by what day of the week they were born on. Beside each line, you will find the meaning of the bolded words.

Line of the poem	Meaning
Monday's child is **fair of face**	is pretty or beautiful
Tuesday's child is **full of grace**	is polite and has good manners
Wednesday's child is **full of woe**	is often sad
Thursday's child **has far to go**	will live long and be successful
Friday's child **works hard for a living**	will always do hard work to earn money
Saturday's child **is loving and giving**	is kind and generous
And the child that is born on the **Sabbath day**	Sunday
Is **bonny and blithe**, and **good and gay**	is beautiful and calm is well behaved and cheerful

a)   On which day of the week were you born? _____

Spelling Week 21 – Words with an *s* Sound Spelled *c* and *s*

Say each word out loud. Listen to the sounds the **c** and **s** make.
Copy and spell each word three times using colours of your choice.

1. plus _____ _____ _____

2. race _____ _____ _____

3. toss _____ _____ _____

4. ice _____ _____ _____

5. sip _____ _____ _____

6. once _____ _____ _____

7. miss _____ _____ _____

8. nice _____ _____ _____

9. same _____ _____ _____

10. circle _____ _____ _____

Spelling Tips

- letter **c** followed by *i, y,* or **e** makes an **s** sound (*city, lacy, pace*)
- letter **s** at the end of a plural word often makes a **z** sound (*eyes*)

circle	ice	miss	nice	once
plus	race	same	sip	toss

1. Fill in the blank using the best spelling word from the list.

a) My brother always likes to have _____ in his drinks.

b) Dad wants to _____ a football around the yard.

c) When I'm home for the summer, I _____ my school friends.

d) Kate and Mike had a _____ from our house to the corner.

e) Grandma likes to sit in the big comfy chair and _____ her tea.

f) The twins like to wear exactly the _____ clothes and shoes.

g) Raj's little sister learned that two _____ two is four.

h) Our silly dog goes around in a _____ chasing her own tail.

i) Most fairy tales start with the words, "_____ upon a time."

j) My woman next door is very _____ to me and my brother.

Spelling Tip

Did you notice anything about the sounds the *c* and *s* make?
In most of these spelling words, both letters make an *s* sound.

1. Write as many words as you can that rhyme with the word below.

   a)   **brace** _____

   b)   **spare** _____

   c)   **cent** _____

   d)   **scuff** _____

2. Write a **c** or an **s** in the space. Make sure the word is spelled correctly.
   Hint: Some words might need more than one letter.

   a)   ___ ity   b) bu ___ y   c) blu ___ h   d) fen ___ e

   e)   me ___   f) i ___ y   g) ba ___ e   h) ___ pend

   i)   ___ kull ___   j) ___ ircu ___   k) cri ___ p   l) whi ___ per

3. A **synonym** is a word that means the same as another word.
   Circle the synonym for the bolded word.

   a)   **stitch**   under   sew   b) **nice**   last   good

4. An **antonym** is a word that has the opposite meaning of another
   word. Circle the antonym for the bolded word.

   a)   **smooth**   rough   shiny   b) **city**   sweep   country

Spelling Week 22 – Words with a Long *u* Sound

Say each word out loud. Look at the letters that make a long *u* sound. Copy and spell each word three times using colours of your choice.

1. cube _____ _____ _____

2. stew _____ _____ _____

3. blue _____ _____ _____

4. mule _____ _____ _____

5. soup _____ _____ _____

6. you _____ _____ _____

7. flew _____ _____ _____

8. true _____ _____ _____

9. chew _____ _____ _____

10. due _____ _____ _____

Spelling Tips: The long **u** sound can be spelled with
- letter *u* followed by a **consonant** + *e* (*use, huge*)
- letter *u* followed by a **consonant** + *i* or *y* (*cupid, duty*)
- letters *ue* (*due*) and *ew* (*chew, few*)

blue	chew	cube	due	flew
mule	soup	stew	true	you

1. Fill in the blank using the best spelling word from the list.

a)   Mom made a yummy beef _____ for dinner.

b)   My library books are _____ back tomorrow.

c)   A bird just _____ into our classroom!

d)   We are having a _____ or false test on Monday.

e)   A _____ is a cross between a horse and a donkey.

f)   Did _____ see Fran's new kittens yet?

g)   We throw vegetables and meat in a pot to make _____.

h)   Our dog likes to _____ on big beef bones.

i)   A square can also be called a _____.

j)   Mandy's favourite colour is _____.

Brain Stretch

How many spelling words can you fit into one sentence and still make sense? Give it a try!

These words with a long **u** sound have been cut apart by mistake! You can help put them back together.

1. Say the first part of the word out loud. Choose a second part. Say it with the first part to see if it makes sense. Draw a line from the first part of the word to the second part. Print the words on the lines at the bottom of the page.

a) tr   ou

b) fr   ew

c) y   ube

d) gr   uit

e) t   ute

f) c   ue

a) _____   b) _____   c) _____

d) _____   e) _____   f) _____

Say each word out loud. What do you notice about the sounds the letters **oi** and **oy** make? Copy and spell each word three times using colours of your choice.

1. join _____ _____ _____

2. boy _____ _____ _____

3. oil _____ _____ _____

4. coin _____ _____ _____

5. loyal _____ _____ _____

6. toy _____ _____ _____

7. noise _____ _____ _____

8. enjoy _____ _____ _____

9. foil _____ _____ _____

10. royal _____ _____ _____

Spelling Tip

Did you notice anything about the sounds that the letters **oi** and **oy** make? Did you notice that they make the same sound?

boy	coin	enjoy	foil	join
loyal	noise	oil	royal	toy

1. Fill in the blank using the best spelling word from the list.

a)   I will put this _____ in my piggybank.

b)   The _____ next door is my best friend.

c)   Mom wrapped corn in _____ to cook on the barbecue.

d)   The baby is sleeping, so we must not make any _____.

e)   This old bunny is my dog Max's favourite _____.

f)   Me and my friends wear paper crowns and pretend we're _____.

g)   We all _____ spending time with our grandparents.

h)   A good friend is a person who is _____ to you.

i)   Dad is getting the _____ changed in the car tomorrow.

j)   Kelly wants to _____ the book club.

Brain Stretch

How many spelling words can you fit into one sentence and still make sense? Give it a try!

1. Use the word list below to look for the words in the puzzle.

   Circle the word in the word search puzzle. Then cross out the word in the list.

S	P	O	I	L	B	A	X	A
O	E	I	D	L	M	N	O	V
Y	R	P	E	C	O	O	Z	O
U	K	J	C	F	I	I	Y	Y
H	W	R	O	U	S	S	O	A
A	H	O	Y	S	T	E	R	G
V	Q	Y	T	F	G	D	F	E
O	Y	A	C	O	I	L	I	H
I	S	L	A	I	K	M	B	J
D	R	F	T	L	Y	U	G	Z

ahoy	avoid	coil	decoy	foil	moist
noise	oyster	royal	soy	spoil	voyage

For these questions, rhyming words do **not** have to be spelled in the same way.

2. Write a word that rhymes with each word below.

   a) **joy** _____   b) **royal** _____   c) **coin** _____

3. Write as many words as you can think of that end in the sound *oil.*

_____

Say each word out loud. Listen for the sounds **ou** and **ow** make.
Copy and spell each word three times using colours of your choice.

1. how _____ _____ _____

2. found _____ _____ _____

3. sour _____ _____ _____

4. about _____ _____ _____

5. town _____ _____ _____

6. shout _____ _____ _____

7. now _____ _____ _____

8. down _____ _____ _____

9. hour _____ _____ _____

10. loud _____ _____ _____

Spelling Tips

Did you notice that the letters **ou** and **ow** often make the same sound? In this lesson, we have used the **ow** sound.

- The letters **ow** can also make a long **o** sound. (*grow*)
- The letters **ou** can also make a short **oo** sound. (*should*)

about	down	found	hour	how
loud	now	shout	sour	town

1. Fill in the blank using the best spelling word from the list.

    a)   Tim is reading a book _____ sharks.

    b)   What was that _____ sound? It scared me!

    c)   I am so tired. I need to go to sleep _____.

    d)   Chris was so far away, I had to _____ to make her hear me.

    e)   Yesterday, I _____ a quarter on the sidewalk.

    f)   I want to learn _____ to make muffins.

    g)   Jessie lives just _____ the street from me.

    h)   We played in the park for a whole _____ today.

    i)   My grandparents live in a very small _____.

    j)   Sam likes to eat _____ gummy worms, but I do not.

Brain Stretch

How many spelling words can you fit into one sentence and still make sense? Give it a try!

1. Ask permission to use a magazine or newspaper for this activity.
   Cut out letters to spell the word below.
   Glue or tape the letters in the correct order in the box.

frown	cloud
towel	snout
pouch	flower

Say each word out loud. Look at the different letters that make an *aw* sound. Copy and spell each word three times using colours of your choice.

1. pause _____ _____ _____

2. straw _____ _____ _____

3. sauce _____ _____ _____

4. hawk _____ _____ _____

5. cause _____ _____ _____

6. hall _____ _____ _____

7. raw _____ _____ _____

8. boss _____ _____ _____

9. draw _____ _____ _____

10. doll _____ _____ _____

Brain Stretch

- Create a word search puzzle based on the spelling words.
- On a piece of paper, write a sentence using each spelling word.

boss	cause	doll	draw	hall
hawk	pause	raw	sauce	straw

1. Fill in the blank using the best spelling word from the list.

   a) We saw two little birds chasing a big _____.

   b) I like apples when they are _____. I don't like them baked.

   c) My dad will _____ the video when my aunt arrives.

   d) Han likes to drink chocolate milk through a _____.

   e) Sara made a cloth _____ for her art project.

   f) We walk in pairs down the _____ at school.

   g) The police tried to find out the _____ of the accident.

   h) My grandmother makes the best tomato _____ ever.

   i) My father's _____ invited my whole family to a barbecue.

   j) I love to _____ pictures of animals.

Brain Stretch

How many spelling words can you fit into one sentence and still make sense? Give it a try!

1. Circle the words that do <u>not</u> have an **aw** sound.

a) flower	caution	laundry	crawl	stall
b) pause	saucer	through	down	comma
c) slow	astronaut	slaw	rough	cause
d) yawn	sound	author	haul	faucet
e) squawk	August	frown	lawn	shower
f) sauce	town	haunt	burn	autumn

2. A **synonym** is a word that means the same as another word. Circle the synonym for the bolded word.

a) **raw**   sour   uncooked   b) **cause**   reason   sneak

3. An **antonym** is a word that has the opposite meaning of another word. Circle the antonym for the bolded word.

a) **thaw**   sink   freeze   b) **awful**   ugly   great

4. What does the word **pause** mean in this sentence?
I had to pause to think about what I wanted to write next.

the feet of an animal   to stop for a short time

Spelling Week 26 – Words with Silent *e*

Say each word out loud. Listen to how the silent **e** makes the vowels sound.Copy and spell each word three times using colours of your choice.

1. rose _____ _____ _____

2. pace _____ _____ _____

3. hike _____ _____ _____

4. tale _____ _____ _____

5. scene _____ _____ _____

6. whale _____ _____ _____

7. ripe _____ _____ _____

8. game _____ _____ _____

9. note _____ _____ _____

10. shape _____ _____ _____

Spelling Tip

For many words that have a vowel followed by a **consonant + silent e**, the **e** makes the vowel say its name.

Spelling Week 26 – Words with Silent *e*

game	hike	note	pace	ripe
rose	scene	shape	tale	whale

1. Fill in the blank using the best spelling word from the list.

a) My favourite fairy _____ is Jack and the Beanstalk.

b) When Sal is in a hurry, he walks at a very fast _____.

c) My friend passed me a _____ about the secret club.

d) Every June, we _____ strawberries at the farm.

e) Everyone was quiet during the exciting movie _____.

f) The largest animal on the planet is the blue _____.

g) Mom's favourite _____ is a pale orange colour.

h) I drew the _____ of a rabbit, but it looked like a duck.

i) Karen's favourite backyard _____ is Obstacle Course.

j) My family loves to _____ in the forest.

Brain Stretch

How many spelling words can you fit into one sentence and still make sense? Give it a try!

Look at the words below. Say the word with a silent *e* out loud. Now say its matching word without the silent *e*. Do you hear the difference in the way the words sound? Adding a silent *e* makes a new word.

1. Draw a line from the word to its meaning.

a) kite   A. way to send a secret message

b) kit   B. faucet

c) code   C. light in colour

d) cod   D. toy on a light frame that is flown in the wind

e) pale   E. strip of sticky material used to hold some thing

f) pal   F. set of things needed for a specific purpose

g) tape   G. type of fish

h) tap   H. friend

2. Write the number words from one to ten that end in silent *e*.

_____

3. For each number word in Question 2, write a word that rhymes with it.

_____

Say each word out loud. Pay attention to which letters you can't hear.
Copy and spell each word three times using colours of your choice.

1. lamb _____ _____ _____

2. knife _____ _____ _____

3. gnome _____ _____ _____

4. night _____ _____ _____

5. calm _____ _____ _____

6. hour _____ _____ _____

7. sign _____ _____ _____

8. walk _____ _____ _____

9. write _____ _____ _____

10. ghost _____ _____ _____

Brain Stretch

- Create a word search puzzle based on the spelling words.
- On a piece of paper, write a sentence using each spelling word.

calm	ghost	gnome	hour	knife
lamb	night	sign	walk	write

1. Fill in the blank using the best spelling word from the list.

   a) Every morning, my mother and I _____ to school together.

   b) Terry wore a _____ costume on Halloween.

   c) Our sheep Daisy has a cute _____ that we named Skipper.

   d) We like to watch for shooting stars in the sky at _____.

   e) The sailboat could not move because the wind was _____.

   f) My mother painted a cheerful _____ to put in the garden.

   g) I use a butter _____ to cut my sandwich.

   h) The store put up a _____ that told about the big sale.

   i) Yu likes to _____ in her journal about things that happen.

   j) It takes an _____ to bake a loaf of banana bread.

Brain Stretch

How many spelling words can you fit into one sentence and still make sense? Give it a try!

You already learned about words with silent **e**. There many more silent letters, as you will see below.

1. Say the word out loud. Underline the letter or letters you can't hear.
   Hint: Some words have more than one silent letter.

   a) knight   b) school   c) lamb   d) half

   e) crumb   f) tone   g) would   h) doubt

   i) knock   j) honest   k) plane   l) dumb

   m) rhyme   n) scene   o) muscle   p) gnome

2. Write all the words from Question 1 that have a silent **b**.

   _____

3. Fill in the missing silent letter or letters.

   a) sal___   b) ___rong   c) ___now   d) ca___m

   e) ___nom___   f) ta___k   g) li___ht   h) ___nif___

Spelling Week 28 – Compound Words

Say each word out loud. Find the two small words that make the bigger word.
Copy and spell each word three times using colours of your choice.

1. into   _____ _____ _____

2. backpack   _____ _____ _____

3. bathtub   _____ _____ _____

4. sunset   _____ _____ _____

5. inside   _____ _____ _____

6. birthday   _____ _____ _____

7. today   _____ _____ _____

8. cupcake   _____ _____ _____

9. bedtime   _____ _____ _____

10. fireman   _____ _____ _____

Brain Stretch

- Create a word search puzzle based on the spelling words.
- On a piece of paper, write a sentence using each spelling word.

backpack	bathtub	bedtime	birthday	cupcake
fireman	inside	into	sunset	today

1. Fill in the blank using the best spelling word from the list.

a) My family likes to sit and watch the _____.

b) Grandma says there is a big surprise _____ this box.

c) We are going to the library _____ to get some books.

d) My favourite treat is a chocolate _____ with sprinkles.

e) We have lots of floating toys to play with in the _____.

f) In the fairy tale, the prince turned _____ a frog.

g) A _____ told our class all about fire safety.

h) Tomorrow there is a party for my cousin's fifth _____.

i) Maya tucked her project carefully into her _____.

j) Rick always tries to stay up past his _____.

Brain Stretch

How many spelling words can you fit into one sentence and still make sense? Give it a try!

Compound words are made by putting two smaller words together to make a bigger word.

Examples: base + ball = baseball   day + light = daylight

1. Write a word that will go with the given word to make a compound word. Say the words together to make sure they make sense. Write the new word on the line.

a)   shoe + _____   _____

b)   _____ + mark   _____

c)   _____ + boat   _____

d)   fire + _____   _____

e)   home + _____   _____

f)   hand + _____   _____

2. Now use the compound words you created to finish this silly story. Write the words in whatever order you wish.

Tara tied her _____ in a knot by accident. She tried

to use a _____ to get it out, but it did not work. She

thought a _____ might work better, but no luck. Tara now

had a _____ _____ that would not

_____, no matter how hard she tried.

Say each word out loud. Pay attention to how **ir** and **ur** sound.
Copy and spell each word three times using colours of your choice.

1. girl _____ _____ _____

2. burn _____ _____ _____

3. first _____ _____ _____

4. dirt _____ _____ _____

5. fur _____ _____ _____

6. curl _____ _____ _____

7. bird _____ _____ _____

8. hurt _____ _____ _____

9. birth _____ _____ _____

10. turn _____ _____ _____

Brain Stretch

- Create a word search puzzle based on the spelling words.
- On a piece of paper, write a sentence using each spelling word.

| bird | birth | burn | curl | dirt |
| first | fur | girl | hurt | turn |

1. Fill in the blank using the best spelling word from the list.

a)   Mom had a headache, so she asked us to _____ the tv down.

b)   Jon fell on the sidewalk and _____ his arm.

c)   If you wear sunscreen, the sun won't _____ your skin.

d)   Working in the garden, we get a lot of _____ on our hands.

e)   Our dog gave _____ to six tiny puppies last night.

f)   There is a pretty blue _____ on our birdbath.

g)   My sister wants to _____ my hair for the party.

h)   It's my _____ to dry the dishes tonight.

i)   My aunt's cat has orange _____ that is thick and soft.

j)   Tomorrow, it is my baby brother's _____ birthday.

Spelling Tip

In many words, the letters *ir*, *ur*, and *er* all make the same sound.

1. Circle the words that do **not** have an *er* sound.

   a)   alert   squirt   their   turn   wear

   b)   hair   gear   churn   dirt   research

2. You are going to decode a secret message! The letters of the alphabet are each represented by a number, as shown below.

1	2	3	4	5	6	7	8	9	10	11	12	13
A	B	C	D	E	F	G	H	I	J	K	L	M

14	15	16	17	18	19	20	21	22	23	24	25	26
N	O	P	Q	R	S	T	U	V	W	X	Y	Z

Write the letter on the line above the number to decode the message.

a) __ __ __ __ __ __ __ __ / __ __ __ / __ __ __ __ __ __ __
   12 5 1 18 14 9 14 7   14 5 23   19 16 5 12 12 9 14 7

__ __ __ __ __ / __ __ / __ __ __ !
23 15 18 4 19   9 19   6 21 14

b) __ __ __ __ / __ / __ __ __ __ __ / __ __ __ / __ __ __ __ __ '
    7 9 22 5   1   19 13 9 12 5   1 14 4   25 15 21 12 12

__ __ __ / __ __ __ / __ __ __ __ .
 7 5 20   15 14 5   2 1 3 11

c)   Make up a secret message and ask a partner to decode it.

Say each word out loud. Watch for the double consonants.
Copy and spell each word three times using colours of your choice.

1. middle _____ _____ _____

2. soccer _____ _____ _____

3. buzz _____ _____ _____

4. silly _____ _____ _____

5. apple _____ _____ _____

6. bottle _____ _____ _____

7. little _____ _____ _____

8. bubble _____ _____ _____

9. grass _____ _____ _____

10. button _____ _____ _____

Brain Stretch

- Create a word search puzzle based on the spelling words.
- On a piece of paper, write a sentence using each spelling word.

| apple | bottle | bubble | button | buzz |
| grass | little | middle | silly | soccer |

1. Fill in the blank using the best spelling word from the list.

   a) My _____ sister is starting to learn to talk.

   b) When I chew gum, I always try to blow a _____.

   c) I have older and younger sisters. I'm the _____ child.

   d) Rena really likes to play _____ every summer.

   e) Grandma made a yummy _____ pie for dessert.

   f) My family likes to watch _____ videos so we can all laugh.

   g) I lost the top _____ off my coat and now my neck is cold.

   h) Dad mows the _____ for our elderly neighbour.

   i) We need a _____ of ketchup for the burgers.

   j) The bees have started to _____ around the new flowers.

Brain Stretch

How many spelling words can you fit into one sentence and still make sense? Give it a try!

1. Write the missing double consonants.

    a) ba____er   b) fo____ow   c) pu____et   d) bo____ow

    e) na____ow   f) sca____er   g) me____y   h) su____y

    i) flu____y   j) sha____ow   k) ki____le   l) da____y

2. Write a word that rhymes with the given word. Change only the first
   letter to make a new word. Make sure the word rhymes.

    a) seek _____   b) look _____   c) bee _____

    d) putter _____   e) bitter _____   f) dill _____

    g) matter _____   h) setter _____   i) tall _____

3. Say the pair of words out loud. Put a checkmark (✔) beside the
   words if the double letters make the same sound. Put an X if the
   double letters do **not** make the same sound.

    a) fool pool ____   b) peel sheet ____   c) look room ____

    d) book stool ____   e) fall mall ____   f) tool wool ____

    g) stoop shook ____   h) smell shell ____   i) skull pull ____

Spelling Week 1 – Test

Name: _____

Listen to the spelling words. Print each spelling word.

1. _____   6. _____

2. _____   7. _____

3. _____   8. _____

4. _____   9. _____

5. _____   10. _____

Bonus

1. _____   2. _____

Spelling Week 2 – Test

Name: _____

Listen to the spelling words. Print each spelling word.

1. _____   6. _____

2. _____   7. _____

3. _____   8. _____

4. _____   9. _____

5. _____   10. _____

Bonus

1. _____   2. _____

Spelling Week 3 – Test

Name: _____

Listen to the spelling words. Print each spelling word.

1. _____   6. _____

2. _____   7. _____

3. _____   8. _____

4. _____   9. _____

5. _____   10. _____

Bonus

1. _____   2. _____

- -

Spelling Week 4 – Test

Name: _____

Listen to the spelling words. Print each spelling word.

1. _____   6. _____

2. _____   7. _____

3. _____   8. _____

4. _____   9. _____

5. _____   10. _____

Bonus

1. _____   2. _____

Spelling Week 5 – Test

Name: _____

Listen to the spelling words. Print each spelling word.

1. _____   6. _____

2. _____   7. _____

3. _____   8. _____

4. _____   9. _____

5. _____   10. _____

Bonus

1. _____   2. _____

Spelling Week 6 – Test

Name: _____

Listen to the spelling words. Print each spelling word.

1. _____   6. _____

2. _____   7. _____

3. _____   8. _____

4. _____   9. _____

5. _____   10. _____

Bonus

1. _____   2. _____

Spelling Week 7 – Test

Name: _____

Listen to the spelling words. Print each spelling word.

1. _____   6. _____

2. _____   7. _____

3. _____   8. _____

4. _____   9. _____

5. _____   10. _____

Bonus

1. _____   2. _____

- -

Spelling Week 8 – Test

Name: _____

Listen to the spelling words. Print each spelling word.

1. _____   6. _____

2. _____   7. _____

3. _____   8. _____

4. _____   9. _____

5. _____   10. _____

Bonus

1. _____   2. _____

Spelling Week 9 – Test

Name: _____

Listen to the spelling words. Print each spelling word.

1. _____   6. _____

2. _____   7. _____

3. _____   8. _____

4. _____   9. _____

5. _____   10. _____

Bonus

1. _____   2. _____

Spelling Week 10 – Test

Name: _____

Listen to the spelling words. Print each spelling word.

1. _____   6. _____

2. _____   7. _____

3. _____   8. _____

4. _____   9. _____

5. _____   10. _____

Bonus

1. _____   2. _____

Spelling Week 11 – Test

Name: _____

Listen to the spelling words. Print each spelling word.

1. _____   6. _____

2. _____   7. _____

3. _____   8. _____

4. _____   9. _____

5. _____   10. _____

Bonus

1. _____   2. _____

- -

Spelling Week 12 – Test

Name: _____

Listen to the spelling words. Print each spelling word.

1. _____   6. _____

2. _____   7. _____

3. _____   8. _____

4. _____   9. _____

5. _____   10. _____

Bonus

1. _____   2. _____

Spelling Week 13 – Test   Name: _____

Listen to the spelling words. Print each spelling word.

1. _____   6. _____

2. _____   7. _____

3. _____   8. _____

4. _____   9. _____

5. _____   10. _____

Bonus

1. _____   2. _____

Spelling Week 14 – Test   Name: _____

Listen to the spelling words. Print each spelling word.

1. _____   6. _____

2. _____   7. _____

3. _____   8. _____

4. _____   9. _____

5. _____   10. _____

Bonus

1. _____   2. _____

Spelling Week 15 – Test

Name: _____

Listen to the spelling words. Print each spelling word.

1. _____   6. _____

2. _____   7. _____

3. _____   8. _____

4. _____   9. _____

5. _____   10. _____

Bonus

1. _____   2. _____

- -

Spelling Week 16 – Test

Name: _____

Listen to the spelling words. Print each spelling word.

1. _____   6. _____

2. _____   7. _____

3. _____   8. _____

4. _____   9. _____

5. _____   10. _____

Bonus

1. _____   2. _____

Spelling Week 17 – Test

Name: _____

Listen to the spelling words. Print each spelling word.

1. _____   6. _____

2. _____   7. _____

3. _____   8. _____

4. _____   9. _____

5. _____   10. _____

Bonus

1. _____   2. _____

Spelling Week 18 – Test

Name: _____

Listen to the spelling words. Print each spelling word.

1. _____   6. _____

2. _____   7. _____

3. _____   8. _____

4. _____   9. _____

5. _____   10. _____

Bonus

1. _____   2. _____

Spelling Week 19 – Test

Name: _____

Listen to the spelling words. Print each spelling word.

1. _____

2. _____

3. _____

4. _____

5. _____

6. _____

7. _____

8. _____

9. _____

10. _____

Bonus

1. _____

2. _____

Spelling Week 20 – Test

Name: _____

Listen to the spelling words. Print each spelling word.

1. _____

2. _____

3. _____

4. _____

5. _____

6. _____

7. _____

8. _____

9. _____

10. _____

Bonus

1. _____

2. _____

Spelling Week 21 – Test   Name: _____

Listen to the spelling words. Print each spelling word.

1. _____   6. _____

2. _____   7. _____

3. _____   8. _____

4. _____   9. _____

5. _____   10. _____

Bonus

1. _____   2. _____

Spelling Week 22 – Test   Name: _____

Listen to the spelling words. Print each spelling word.

1. _____   6. _____

2. _____   7. _____

3. _____   8. _____

4. _____   9. _____

5. _____   10. _____

Bonus

1. _____   2. _____

Spelling Week 23 – Test   Name: _____

Listen to the spelling words. Print each spelling word.

1. _____   6. _____

2. _____   7. _____

3. _____   8. _____

4. _____   9. _____

5. _____   10. _____

Bonus

1. _____   2. _____

Spelling Week 24 – Test   Name: _____

Listen to the spelling words. Print each spelling word.

1. _____   6. _____

2. _____   7. _____

3. _____   8. _____

4. _____   9. _____

5. _____   10. _____

Bonus

1. _____   2. _____

Spelling Week 25 – Test

Name: _____

Listen to the spelling words. Print each spelling word.

1. _____   6. _____

2. _____   7. _____

3. _____   8. _____

4. _____   9. _____

5. _____   10. _____

Bonus

1. _____   2. _____

Spelling Week 26 – Test

Name: _____

Listen to the spelling words. Print each spelling word.

1. _____   6. _____

2. _____   7. _____

3. _____   8. _____

4. _____   9. _____

5. _____   10. _____

Bonus

1. _____   2. _____

Spelling Week 27 – Test

Listen to the spelling words. Print each spelling word.

1. _____

2. _____

3. _____

4. _____

5. _____

6. _____

7. _____

8. _____

9. _____

10. _____

Bonus

1. _____

2. _____

Spelling Week 28 – Test

Name: _____

Listen to the spelling words. Print each spelling word.

1. _____

2. _____

3. _____

4. _____

5. _____

6. _____

7. _____

8. _____

9. _____

10. _____

Bonus

1. _____

2. _____

Spelling Week 29 – Test

Name: _____

Listen to the spelling words. Print each spelling word.

1. _____ 6. _____

2. _____ 7. _____

3. _____ 8. _____

4. _____ 9. _____

5. _____ 10. _____

Bonus

1. _____ 2. _____

Spelling Week 30 – Test

Name: _____

Listen to the spelling words. Print each spelling word.

1. _____ 6. _____

2. _____ 7. _____

3. _____ 8. _____

4. _____ 9. _____

5. _____ 10. _____

Bonus

1. _____ 2. _____

Spelling Practice Menu

Colour Code Write out your spelling words using one colour for the vowels and another colour for the consonants.	**Rainbow Words** Write out your spelling words into the shape of a rainbow using the colours of the rainbow.	**Hidden Words** Draw a picture outline. Add your spelling words to the picture so they are "hiding." Colour your picture.
Cut It Out! Cut letters out of a magazine. Spell out your words and glue them onto a sheet of paper.	**Word Search** Create a word search based on your spelling words.	**Rhyming Words** Write out your spelling words with a rhyming word next to each spelling word.
Alphabetical Order Print your spelling words in alphabetical order.	**Spelling Word Typing** Type your spelling words on a computer or other device.	**Magnetic Letter Words** Use magnetic letters to make your spelling words.
Spelling Race How many times can you write out your spelling words in three minutes?	**Sort It Out** Sort your spelling words into categories of your choice and record them on a piece of paper.	**Spelling Word Fun** Form your spelling words using: • modelling clay • pipe cleaners • toothpicks

Everyday Words to Know How to Spell

The Fry word list contains the most common words used in English listed in order of frequency and includes all parts of speech.

the	or	will	number
of	one	up	no
and	had	other	way
a	by	about	could
to	words	out	people
in	but	many	my
is	not	then	than
you	what	them	first
that	all	these	water
it	were	so	been
he	we	some	called
was	when	her	who
for	your	would	oil
on	can	make	sit
are	said	like	now
as	there	him	find
with	use	into	long
his	an	time	down
they	each	has	day
I	which	look	did
at	she	two	get
be	do	more	come
this	how	write	made
have	their	go	may
from	if	see	part

Everyday Words to Know How to Spell

The Fry word list contains the most common words used in English listed in order of frequency and includes all parts of speech.

over	say	set	try
new	great	put	kind
sound	where	end	hand
take	help	does	picture
only	through	another	again
little	much	well	change
work	before	large	off
know	line	must	play
place	right	big	spell
years	too	even	air
live	means	such	away
me	old	because	animal
back	any	turn	house
give	same	here	point
most	tell	why	page
very	boy	ask	letter
after	follow	went	mother
things	came	men	answer
our	want	read	found
just	show	need	study
name	also	land	still
good	around	different	learn
sentence	form	home	should
man	three	us	world
think	small	move	

Write a silly story using as many spelling words as you can. Draw a picture.

_____

_____

_____

_____

_____

_____

_____

I checked for: ☐ capitals and end marks ☐ correct spelling ☐ neat printing

_____'s **Word Search**

Create a word search and share it with someone.

Word List

Spelling Tracker

Name	Week __	Week __	Week __	Week __	Week __	Week __	Week __	Week __	Week __	Week __	Week __	Week __	Week __	Week __	Week __

Spelling Week 1 – Words with a Short *a* Sound, pp. 2–3
1. a) and b) can c) pan d) sat e) yam f) lap g) cap h) hat i) jam j) had

Spelling Week 1 – Word Study, p. 4
1. a) hat b) sat c) had d) jam e) cap f) and g) pan h) yam i) lap j) can
2. a) jam, yam b) can, pan c) hat, sat d) cap, lap

Spelling Week 2 – Words with a Short *i* Sound, pp. 5–6
1. a) big b) fix c) win d) if e) pit f) his g) dig h) pin i) will j) him

Spelling Week 2 – Word Study, p. 7
1. a) big, fig, rig b) will, spill, bill c) pin, skin, win d) pit, mitt e) fix, mix f) fizz, his, whiz
2. a) large b) mend c) hole d) tack
3. a) tiny b) lose c) break d) hill

Spelling Week 3 – Words with a Short *o* Sound, pp. 8–9
1. a) dog b) fog c) lost d) hot e) job f) off g) onto h) stop i) cob j) box
You may wish to ask children what job they want to do when they grow up.

Spelling Week 3 – Word Study, p. 10
1. a) ob; cob b) f; off c) to; stop d) o, t; lost e) o, t; onto f) b; box g) o; job h) og; fog
2. a) pot b) sock c) toss d) stop e) fox f) doll

Spelling Week 4 – Words with a Short *u* Sound, pp. 11–12
1. a) run b) cut c) hug d) must e) up f) fun g) jug h) bus i) but j) us

Spelling Week 4 – Word Study, p. 13
1. a) cough, tune b) round, bounce c) pounce, beauty d) grouch, guess e) comb, about
2. a) lumber b) cover c) rough d) judge e) fluff f) bump g) touch h) bubble

Spelling Week 5 – Words with a Short *e* Sound, pp. 14–15
1. a) went b) bed c) end d) tell e) best f) wet g) yes h) red i) let j) leg

Spelling Week 5 – Word Study, p. 16
1. a) better b) bread c) shed d) mend e) said
2. a) went b) best c) read d) neck e) set f) fence

Spelling Week 6 – Words with a Long *a* Sound, pp. 17–18
1. a) stay b) wait c) page d) game e) save f) sale g) Today h) play i) take j) rain

Answers

Spelling Week 6 – Word Study, p. 19

1. a) break, late, wait b) lace, hazy, crate c) waste, grape, face d) sway, make, grey g) may, gate, eight

2. A, J, K

3. 8, 18, 28, 38, 48, 58, 68, 78, 80, 81, 82, 83, 84, 85, 86, 87, 88, 89, 98

4. Sample answers: ray, hay, may, say, lay, way, pray, fray, grey, stay, slay, tray, sleigh, spray, away

Spelling Week 7 – Words with a Long e Sound, pp. 20–21

1. a) meet b) need c) three d) read e) mean f) keep g) each h) easy i) dream j) eat

Spelling Week 7 – Word Study, p. 22

1. a) bee, flea, tea b) meat, wheat, fleet c) team, seem, beam d) heat, street, sheet, seat e) feel, meal, seal f) reef, leaf, thief

2. a) unkind b) munch c) small d) go

3. a) sour b) strong c) messy d) above

4. a) 2 syllables b) 1 syllable c) 3 syllables

Spelling Week 8 – Words with a Long i Sound, pp. 23–24

1. a) right b) bite c) time d) pie e) tight f) write g) pine h) kind i) high j) night

Spelling Week 8 – Word Study, p. 25

1. a) spine, guy, fly b) time, kind, iron c) ripe, eye d) mine, grime, twice, while e) rind, wipe f) lime, rhyme, lie

2. a) fine b) time c) eye d) line e) sunshine f) climb

4. five, nine

Spelling Week 9 – Words with y as Long i and Long e Sounds, pp. 26–27

1. a) try b) story c) very d) why e) only f) fly g) many h) any i) baby j) cry

Spelling Week 9 – Word Study, p. 28

1. a) only b) story c) cry d) fly e) very f) try

2. a) fry + pan b) day + time c) horse + fly d) jelly + bean e) eye + ball f) sun + set

Spelling Week 10 – Words with a Long o Sound, pp. 29–30

1. snow b) follow c) also d) glow e) soap f) throw g) road h) nose i) goal j) hope

Spelling Week 10 – Word Study, p. 31
1. a) tower, clock b) sock, work c) book, toss d) pool, slop
2. Sample answers a) tore, more, sore, bore, pore, fore, wore, gore b) boat, coat, goat, float c) bow, low, tow, glow, crow, throw, follow, swallow, pillow, borrow, tomorrow d) port, fort, sort, sport, short
3. a) 2 syllables b) 3 syllables c) 1 syllable
4. nowhere, snowflake, popcorn

Spelling Week 11 – Words with Long and Short *oo* Sounds, pp. 32–33
1. a) crew b) school c) should d) threw e) took f) soon g) book h) cook i) food j) clue

Spelling Week 11 – Word Study, p. 34
1. a) flew, boom, due b) room, fruit, boot c) tool, flute, mood d) bloom, rule, soup
2. a) look, soot, wool b) stood, foot, shook c) brook, book d) wood, crook, could
3. a) S b) L c) L d) S e) L f) L g) L h) S i) L j) S k) L l) S

Spelling Week 12 – Words in the *ar* Family, pp. 35–36
1. a) barn b) card c) mark d) dark e) yard f) star g) hard h) bark i) party j) farm

Spelling Week 12 – Word Study, p. 37
1) a) apart b) card c) far d) hare e) park f) sharp
2. Sample answers: a) I take care of my pet rabbit every day. b) I like to share my snacks with my friends. c) I saw a big shark at the aquarium. d) I read part of my new book this morning. e) Our neighbour has a very large dog named Max. f) My mother says it's not polite to stare. g) My brother wears a mouth guard when he plays hockey.

Spelling Week 13 – Words with *s* Blends, pp. 38–39
1. a) still b) snack c) smart d) skip e) smell f) just g) spill h) slip i) swim j) scarf

Spelling Week 13 – Word Study, p. 40
1. Sample answers: a) skin, skip, skim, skill, skit, skate, skimp, ask, task, risk, whisk b) slim, slit, slot, slip, slam, slap, slash, slang, sling, slack, hassle c) smash, smack, smart, smatter, smell d) spa, spin, span, spar, speck, spend, spell, spark, spill, spank, splash, spatter, sparkle, splatter, splinter e) scan, scam, scar, scat, scare, scarf, school, scatter, scared, scald f) swim, swam, swift, swing, swill, swell, swish, sweet, sweat, sweater, swelter, swollen g) stay, stun, stem, star, stamp, stick, stern, staff, stiff, sting, stunk, stark, start, strap, best, vest, just, past, last, mast, cast, rust, must, trust, worst, first, fist, wrist, castle, wrestle h) snap, snip, snit, snot, snack, snick, sniff
2. a) st b) sn c) sk d) sl e) sw f) sp g) sn h) st
3. a) extra b) begin
4. a) stick b) brave

Spelling Week 14 – Words with _r_ Blends, pp. 41–42
1. a) tree b) grab c) pretty d) trip e) from f) bring g) crab h) brush i) drip j) frog

Spelling Week 14 – Word Study, p. 43
You may wish to create a bulletin board display of children's pictures or drawings.

Spelling Week 15 – Words in the _sh_ Family, pp. 44–45
1. a) shell b) trash c) share d) dish e) wish f) brush g) washer h) push i) shake j) fresh

Spelling Week 15 – Word Study, p. 46
You may wish to create a bulletin board display of children's pages, or have children share their pages with a partner.

Spelling Week 16 – Words in the _ck_ Family, pp. 47–48
1. a) pick b) rock c) quack d) deck e) pack f) clock g) sock h) flick i) luck j) neck

Spelling Week 16 – Word Study, p. 49
You may wish to create a bulletin board display of children's drawings

Spelling Week 17 – Words in the _th_ and _wh_ Families, pp. 50–51
1. a) That b) What c) both d) there e) those f) Who g) When h) Which i) Where j) This

Spelling Week 17 – Word Study, p. 52
1. a) Who b) Why c) When d) How e) Which f) What g) Where
2. a) there b) Then c) These d) That e) this f) those

Spelling Week 18 – Words in the _ch_ and _tch_ Families, pp. 53–54
1. a) match b) chick c) Watch d) witch e) much f) chin g) chat h) lunch i) catch j) watch

Spelling Week 18 – Word Study, p. 55
1. **_ch_** words: chance, chill, crunch, finch, march, munch, pinch, ranch; **_tch_** words: hatch, latch, match, patch, pitch, sketch, stitch, watch
2. shout, month, where

Spelling Week 19 – Number Words, pp. 56–57
1. a) one b) six c) ten, ten d) seven e) ten f) three g) two h) eight i) five j) nine

Spelling Week 19 – Word Study, p. 58
1. a) four, seven, eleven, thirteen, twenty b) one, five, nine, twelve, seventeen
2. a) eight, fourteen, nine, six, twenty b) eighteen, five, nineteen, sixteen, two

Spelling Week 20 – Days of the Week, pp. 59–60
1. a) Friday b) Wednesday c) morning d) Saturday e) Tuesday f) afternoon g) Sunday h) Night i) Thursday j) Monday

Spelling Week 20 – Word Study, p. 61
Discuss the poem with children and stress that it was a very old belief that people no longer have. It is simply a fun nursery rhyme. If they don't know which day they were born on, ask them to find out from their parents for the next day. You may wish to ask a few children which day they were born on, or make a tally chart on the board to see how many were born on each specific day. You may also wish to point out that the word "gay" is an old word that means cheerful or happy.

Spelling Week 21 – Words with an *s* Sound Spelled *c* and *s*, pp. 62–63
1. a) ice b) toss c) miss d) race e) sip f) same g) plus h) circle i) Once j) nice

Spelling Week 21 – Word Study, p. 64
1. Sample answers: a) pace, face, case, lace, race, trace, grace b) tear, fair, fare, bear, lair, care, rare, scare, prayer c) meant, lent, spent, bent d) cuff, buff, fluff, scruff, gruff, tough, rough, enough
2. a) city b) busy c) blush d) fence e) mess f) icy g) base h) spend i) skulls j) circus k) crisp l) whisper
3. a) sew b) good
4. a) rough b) country

Spelling Week 22 – Words with a Long *u* Sound, pp. 65–66
1. a) stew b) due c) flew d) true e) mule f) you g) soup h) chew i) cube j) blue

Spelling Week 22 – Word Study, p. 67
1. a) true b) fruit c) you d) grew e) tube f) cute

Spelling Week 23 – Words in the *oi* and *oy* Families, pp. 68–69
1. a) coin b) boy c) foil d) noise e) toy f) royal g) enjoy h) loyal i) oil j) join

Spelling Week 23 – Word Study, p. 70

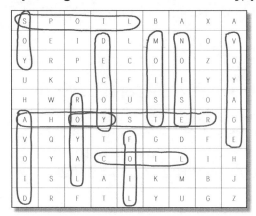

2. Sample answers: a) joy, boy, soy, annoy b) loyal, oil, soil, coil, toil c) join
3. Sample answers: coil, foil, boil, soil, royal, loyal, spoil

Spelling Week 24 – Words in the *ou* and *ow* Families, pp. 71–72
1. a) about b) loud c) now d) shout e) found f) how g) down h) hour i) town j) sour

Spelling Week 24 – Word Study, p. 73
You may wish to create a bulletin board display of children's pages.

Spelling Week 25 – Words in the *aw* Family, pp. 74–75
1. a) hawk b) raw c) pause d) straw e) doll f) hall g) cause h) sauce i) boss j) draw

Spelling Week 25 – Word Study, p. 76
1. a) flower b) through, down c) slow, rough d) sound e) frown, shower f) town, burn
2. a) uncooked b) reason
3. a) freeze b) great
4. to stop for a short time

Spelling Week 26 – Words with Silent *e*, pp. 77–78
1. a) tale b) pace c) note d) ripe e) scene f) whale g) rose h) shape i) game j) hike

Spelling Week 26 – Word Study, p. 79
1. a) D b) F c) A d) G e) C f) H g) E h) B
2. one, five, nine
3. Sample answers: **one**: fun, run, sun, ton; **five**: live, dive, alive, drive, arrive, thrive; **nine**: fine, mine, line, wine, sign, swine

Spelling Week 27 – More Silent Letters, pp. 80–81
1. a) walk b) ghost c) lamb d) night e) calm f) gnome g) knife h) sign i) write j) hour

Answers

Spelling Week 27 – Word Study, p. 82
1. a) k and g b) h c) b d) l e) b f) e g) l h) b i) k and c j) h k) e l) b m) h and e n) c and e o) c and e p) g and e
2. lamb, crumb, dumb
3. a) e; sale b) w; wrong c) k; know d) l; calm e) g and e f) l; talk g) g; light h) k and e; knife

Spelling Week 28 – Compound Words, pp. 83–84
1. a) sunset b) inside c) today d) cupcake e) bathtub f) into g) fireman h) birthday i) backpack j) bedtime

Spelling Week 28 – Word Study, p. 85
1. Sample answers: a) shoelace, shoeshine b) bookmark, checkmark c) sailboat, tugboat d) fireplace, fireman, fireworks e) homemade, homegrown, homeland f) handmade, handshake, handprint
2. You may wish to have children share their silly stories with the class, or create a bulletin board display of their stories. As an extension of this activity, you could give children 5 or 6 short words to create compound words from, or they can think of compound words by themselves. Children can then use those words to write a silly short story of their own to share with the class.

Spelling Week 29 – Words in the *ir* and *ur* Families, pp. 86–87
1. a) turn b) hurt c) burn d) dirt e) birth f) bird g) curl h) turn i) fur j) first

Spelling Week 29 – Word Study, p. 88
1. a) their, wear b) hair, gear
2. a) Learning new spelling words is fun! b) Give a smile and you'll get one back. c) You may wish to have students share their secret messages with another partner or in a group of four. Alternatively, you can ask volunteers for their secret message code, write it on the board, and decode the message as a class.

Spelling Week 30 – Words with Double Consonants, pp. 89–90
1. a) little b) bubble c) middle d) soccer e) apple f) funny g) button h) grass i) bottle j) buzz

Spelling Week 30 – Word Study, p. 91
1. a) tt; batter b) ll; follow c) pp; puppet d) rr; borrow e) rr; narrow f) tt; scatter g) ss; messy h) nn; sunny i) ff; fluffy j) ll; shallow k) bb; kibble l) dd; daddy
2. Sample answers: a) week, peek, leek b) book, took c) see, tee, fee, wee d) butter, gutter e) sitter, fitter, quitter f) pill, will, sill, bill, fill g) batter, fatter, patter h) better, letter, wetter i) fall, mall, ball, wall
3. a) ✔ b) ✔ c) X d) X e) ✔ f) X g) X h) ✔ i) X

Great Work!
Spelling Superstar

_____

Amazing Effort!
Spelling Superstar

_____